EDITOR-IN-CHIEF
Alan Fox

EDITOR
Timothy Green

LOGO DESIGN
David Navas

ASSISTANT EDITOR
Megan Green

COVER ART
David Swartz
"Yellow Moon"

EDITOR EMERITUS
Stellasue Lee

PROOFREADING
Jeffrey Gerretse

© 2020 by The Rattle Foundation

Rattle Young Poets Anthology, 2020

www.Rattle.com

CONTENTS

2020

Note on the Cover Artist

David Swartz is a Lisbon-based artist from Toronto, Canada, who envisions the artist's hands' in action as the veritable subject of art in all its multiple forms.

www.davidswartzart.com

Young Poets

Caroline Blumer

ORANGES

Today my mother said that she liked the smell of oranges.
She said, look how good this sounds:
my hair smells like oranges,
my father grows oranges in California,
my mother eats oranges in the afternoon. But I knew
that my mother would never eat oranges in the afternoon,
would never eat an orange while

there was a grapefruit. Knew she would never
call her father in California if he lived there
because California is fake.
She knows herself she doesn't smell her own hair,
and she doesn't care what she puts in it.
She knows it's not about the brand,
it's about the purpose behind the brand.

She knows that oranges aren't as healthy, that if
you have diabetes, you'll die sooner than someone
else. She knows that the cookies
at Walmart are chalky and filled with sugar.
That there is protein in cheese, that
one daughter is tired, and the other
won't settle down.

She has anxiety, but refuses to admit it,
says that counting to yourself
is normal. She complains all the time how teens are
stuck and can't think right. Says I am a teenager.
Knows that I work ambitiously,
knows that when I think wrongly, I know that I am wrong.

She knows that I don't listen. She knows that I'm a faker
at home, that I like Dad more. That I will

[...]

one day leave the house and drink
from a keg at three in the morning.

She looks at my body and knows that A-line dresses
look better on me because I am short.
She tells me that I have an oval
face, tells me to eat Greek yogurt and exercise more. Says I
look greedy for attention when I wear those clothes. She tells
me You smile nice. Tells me that I don't smile enough.

Taught me to smile while I sing, taught me to cross my legs,
taught me to be scared, taught me that being anxious
is part of living. Told me that I better listen to her, because she's
        been around.
Tells me that I might die one day from being fat
if I don't move, tells me that I'm not ladylike,
to stop putting on makeup. Tells me that if I
moisturized I wouldn't have wrinkles. Tells me don't settle, fight.

She tells me oranges are for the sweet kind
of people who pretend to love their mothers. Oranges
won't tell you what's wrong.

Ellie Bodeman

FIFTEEN THINGS I LEARNED FROM INSIDE A PSYCHIATRIC WARD

What the words "Code Grey" meant

How to protect myself

Take your meds

About the holes in the walls

Don't wear shoelaces, have zippers or strings

To share how you got there

To tell the same story over and over again to the caseworkers

Listen

Take it all in

Don't eat the food

Don't overshare or you'll get a longer stay

The word "Coping"

Cover your wrists

Talk less

Stop.

Clara Collins

SELF-PORTRAIT AS BRITNEY SPEARS SHAVING HER HEAD

They sold her hair on eBay.
That night, the air whittled to a ruddy peak
and she's driving, hurtling up that truck ramp
to the overpass where the stars hang
like icicles. There's a plastic-red ICEE
in the cup holder, the gas station
tile slick under her feet.
There's a flash of man-made light.
And there's an electric buzz—
the soundtrack to the furious juxtaposition
of a woman and her voice, the deciduous spin
of embitterment. Infamy tastes
like a Pixie Stick made of cigarette ash.

My dance teacher used to tell us
to watch ourselves like the audience would.
So I became the mirrors lining the wall,
surrounded by myself at each turn
until I got so tired I quit.
Just having a body seemed
like a statement. I tried drawing myself
out of my skin, clawing at my stomach
like a pearl was waiting inside,
never realizing the forced exodus
was nothing new. They got it wrong—

it wasn't reinvention.
It was the eclipse of all her loose selves.
I'd like to ask her what it's like
existing in so many places at once.

See, she's tangible now, untouchable.
The hair stays in her hands
even as it falls on the floor.

E.E. Colmenares

WOMAN TO GIRL

Put the water in the pan before you heat up the pan; salt the water before you put the pasta in; turn your jeans inside out to keep their color; if you fall down get back up; never pick up a coin on the ground—money is disgusting; don't brag in front of the less fortunate; if you know the right answer then raise your hand, even if you want to hide your knowledge; tell someone if they have something in their teeth; *even if it's my principal?*; hold your head high no matter what; don't back down if you're right; if someone's acting like an idiot look at them as such; no, not your principal, your friend or your enemy, not superior; if there is a pyramid of fruit do not pick from the middle or bottom; at Halloween let the little kids get two pieces; always have faith in yourself; if someone backs you into a corner, there is always a way out; this is how to make popcorn; this is how to comfort your friends; don't be friends with someone you only like half of the time; watch what you wear to church events—even if it's a campout; give and receive credit where credit is due; if the offer isn't right, walk away; this is how to conserve energy; this is how to stay warm in winter; this is how to wash your bra; don't go to a school that has the same name as a poultry company—if you can help it; know your audience; even if you have shorts on under a skirt don't test it; build people up and knock down those who are as big as skyscrapers; try your best; practice how you're going to play; if it doesn't fit, it doesn't fit; get help before you need it; zip up zippers before you wash— sounds less scary; don't buy something just to buy it; find your passion and never let go of it; this is how you decline an invitation to the dance; this is what you wear to a school dance; this is what you wear to a church dance; this is what you wear to a gala; if you have a loud voice, own it; if you get something wrong fix it, even if it doesn't change your grade; do something because you want to, not because you have to—even if it's a requirement and you have to make up something completely untrue; this is how to hold your head high in the face of shame; if you can't drink at your wedding, then you're too young to get married; this is how to walk the runway; *I wouldn't want to marry a stinky boy anyway!*; don't go camping without layers; always think before you talk—unless they deserve it; if your friend has something in their teeth, tell them!; date someone for at least four seasons before marrying them; if you don't want to wear white on your wedding day, you don't have to; if you can't find what you're looking for never stop believing in what you want; do not wear flip-flops in the city; "ma'am" should stay in the South with your elders; be yourself even when everyone is watching; don't look down; live in the present, not the past; this is how to let go of revenge fantasies; this is how to embrace the world and its dark corners; this is how to make a simple treat on a cold day; don't question your actions, even if they're wrong—just learn from them and move on; live simply or lavishly, just live your way; break a rule every once in a while; have fun, even during a standardized test; write your own narrative, don't be influenced by my achievements or life decisions; remember, I want to be buried naturally, don't even think about cremating me.

Bella Cosentino

GOLDEN SHOVEL: SELF-PORTRAIT IN FOURTH GRADE

after David Graham, "Self-Portrait with Self-Doubt"

Some Tuesdays, when bordering ourselves at
What I named the dusty turf, leaves were pulled on the
Small twisters we threw plastic jewelry into while the playground
Sagged a little. It never was awfully hot or sticky, as

Going to wait inside the hallway was too close to a
Retreat. Since the metal tube slide gave one shorts-wearing boy
A burn, handfuls of sand were flung inside to comfort while I
Pressed my arms against my sides and hoped nobody saw

When I winced. There wasn't much to show for myself,
None of us had to ride the witch's hat or stay in
Place on the trapeze rings with sliding hands, those
Rings still out of reach from the kids

I liked to watch when it got boring. The teachers,
Only sitting in the shade, called
Or hollered at the jungle gym kids, kids who felt special
When their name was heard over fumbling feet and those

Cranky springs under the colored horses smiling like dolts.
It's not very easy to remember the faces of those
Who I helped on the monkey bars, or the chumps
That promised to catch when my hands would stumble, those

Were nice. They're attractive now, the harebrains
I won't recognize the same, appearing once in a while and
Fizzing off as orange sodas I used to drink, babbling
Onto my tongue as though explaining through fuzzy fragments.

Emerson Davis-Martin

SHRIMP HEARTS ARE IN THEIR HEADS

My mom told me last night
a shrimp's heart lives
in its head.
You're the same way,
she says stroking my hair.

Small prawns shuffle
as they carry coral abdomens.
Long antennae graze the ocean floor,
cloudy eyes like fogged mirrors.

Two sides wade in treacherous waters,
I stand in the middle,
a tug of war.

I search for my mom,
my head pounding,
blood boiling like molten lava.
As I tread across the wet sand,
it weighs down my feet,
sticking to my shell-like glue.

I watch as oxygen sways
through the water
like wind shuffles leaves.
My body quivers from the cold.

I have two options
and I can't find my mom.
I have two options.

I turn right.

Mya De La Rosa

ANOTHER DAY, ANOTHER DESTINY

Favelas that I could not see slide down
In the mud of my memories, clanking
Tin roofs I slew past because
A frothy mouthed dog or a bubbly boy
Might steal my heart—it's hollow anyway.

Favelas of different names are
Eluding my grasp because they aren't mine.

While hustling to the bus stop skirts sway close,
Nahuatl legs and culture swelter
Bloody around the bend in our poor minds.

Tío Boy, like a dry leaf, whisks away
In the dizzy breeze, protecting his dogs.
He shits in a bucket on Nina's porch
Because he needs money on the cracked streets
Where kids play, under sneakers, with caged birds.

Pero yo no soy guey, yo soy fresa.
And the white boys preach, "Liberty!" all day
While I write. My daddy gave me more.
Gave me more to know and more to work for.

Far, home is a lonely place without me.
Haze sticks there, so I'm looking to the path.
The forks, worn or smooth, will make me mighty.

I'll wait for the women and men, just now.
Shine the star for my sailor eyes to sail
These glass waters to new worlds.

Nina Evans

SURVIVING THE APOCALYPSE

Ever since Parkland,
My parents have been waking up early
To see me before I catch the bus.
This is love in the apocalypse.

A couple months ago,
We didn't know it was a drill.
I exchanged fearful glances with people I've never liked.
This is solidarity in the apocalypse.

The news tells us
Earth has ten years to live.
I say to Mom, "There go your grandkids."
This is laughter in the apocalypse.

I always wondered how the people in the disaster movies could
        think they stood a chance.
But I've seen us rise to the occasion as the tides rise to our shores.

And if our city ever drowns,
Covered in gallons of our mistakes,
We will learn to swim.
This is surviving the apocalypse.

C.A. Harper

FOUR HAIKU

dark night
men interrupting
the silence

late days
outgrown my
grownup's costume

butterfly
the rain
still happens

just the view
water flowing down
the silent stream

THE DRESS

The apples and the roses take the pink.
The lilies and the grapes take the purple.
The crabs and the sky take the blue.
And that is why the dress is yellow.

Sarah Lao

FIRELIGHT

April & I fist the days as if
      the calendar's pages were the ruffles
on my sundress. I dress the nicks
      on my jaw with springs & hands.
Undress & redress. Make it tick
      in time with the neighbor's world
clock. Let me tell you again about
      last Tuesday, when Mama had me
cut her bangs straight across,
      the split ends forming all the dodged
questions left over on the floor.
      Look, the living room is so full
of old takeout and fossils. How
      honest. In another life, I imagine
the bones must discover themselves
      in a sheath of blubber & teach me
how to backstroke. Feel the river's
      slow pulse & the slick of fish
coiling around me like twine.
      I confess: I want to touch my body
in the dark. Hands empty & gullible.
      To play cartographer & mark the
frontline of every frontier with
      red flags. Should I rewind. Should
I stop the mailman. Should I pick
      up the landline. Then maybe this time
I'll see the lightning before
      it hits the prairie. Or the back-
hand before its crack.
      Either way, this house will
overturn as the cosmos spirals
      on its axis. The alarm

clocks will trip & shatter
       & I will be left holding
onto nothing but my dazed
       sundress. Here we are,
the ground in splinters
       of kindling, soot tracking
the grass. Watch: this sky
       blemished. This field.
Our two bodies—
       everything burning
like it was meant to.

Cassidy Lewis

TO BUILD A MOTHER WHO STANDS LIKE A HOUSE

"Love your neighbor as yourself."
—*Galatians 5:14*

I think if God and I lived in a house together, we'd never
really sleep. Because I would want to ask a thousand
questions and God would want to listen, droopy eyed
in the corner of my bedroom, head tilted to the side
to make like He was drifting off. Eating fruit from Eve's
tree to stay awake, floating on a hammock of clouds,
hands tucked together, like the house He's built for us
is Heaven. But if you and God lived in a house,

it would be constructed by Solomon and Isaiah and Josh,
written onto the street as if it was the books of the Old
Testament, and you'd keep the doors shut because nobody
should come inside. I think the two of you would eat supper
together in the dining room and God would storytell
about Heaven. About how it breathes, the way it opens
and closes like the wings on and off of an Angel's back.
You are my mother but the night you introduced me

to Jesus, I met His eyes and the words felt wrong. I imagine
God as a hotel. As the different suites He could be, the furniture.
As the little yellow lights that reflect off balcony windows
during the night time. Think of Him as the swimming pool,
as the water, the tile. Bath linen, bed. Imagine Him as the wood
of a reception desk, as the receptionist. A keycard held in each palm
to hand to His guests. I'd like to see this God. Like to touch
Him how you touch the silver crucifix of Jesus hanging

above my nightstand. His hips curled in, lean. Hold Him
while you preach to me about love and hate and all the things
that fill us. The things that curate sin. Pride, envy, anger.
This is where I write we disagree. Because while your door
may close for the people you dislike in God's name, His will
remain open. Yours is steeled shut, and His is revolving,
and mine is thin and transparent like glass. I sit in Church
and look at God standing on the stage by the pastor. A reminder
that He sees and loves everybody. That He too doesn't want

closed-mindedness in our religion. And maybe you don't see God
but His shadow, where it slips behind the stage curtains to hide.
Less God and more silhouette. I think He wouldn't buy a house,
but build one. And it'd be made the same way He is. Bare footed,
sheet wrapped from shoulders to hips. Tall, head peeking down
at the two of us from His home up in Heaven. A knowing smile
growing from His thin lips. Pull off the road, I know that you're tired.
Come to the hotel, there's a room for you waiting.

Layla Linnard

US THREE

I liked it a few months ago
It was just us three
There was no sharing my room
There was no screaming baby
I at least slept when
It was just us three

It was just us three
I at least slept when
There was no screaming baby
There was no sharing my room
It was just us three
I liked it a few months ago

Sarah Mohammed

عيد الأضحى (EID AL-AHDA)

Eid Mubarak

The gentle blessing floats off our tongues like
shallow breaths, as morning dew from the grass kisses our bare feet.

We gather in unity; we are one on this holy morning.
Umma starts the ترتيل (Tarteel) that materializes into our faith.

We rise together, voices mangled with accents, dressed with youth
and age, we combine
into the rich and powerful tajwid of worship.

We are no longer reciting. Our hearts sing with love and devotion
to ourselves, each other and our beliefs, blending

into the burning drop of light rising slowly
above us, streaks of deep color across delicate morning blue.

The prayers end. We nourish ourselves with hand-cooked meals.
We can taste them before bringing the food to our lips.

A leaf rustles. No one dares disturb our sanctuary
blessed by Mother Nature herself on our celebration, our Eid,
but we were wrong,

A mob came in our place of worship and
screamed slurs
They waved their tattered cardboard signs in our faces
our clasped hands our beating hearts
we looked at other faces they could wreck us
it was our time to be united to be pure and true
we are Americans anyway why should we "leave Americans alone"

[...]

we were born in the valleys of this country in the patterns
of practice Eid Mubarak

The gentle blessing floats off our tongues like shallow breaths
as we huddle together in tightly packed rows against the sticky
linoleum floors of my uncle's apartment

Harkiran (Kiran) Narula

HARDEEP

papa has told me this story so many times.
he was young and in the bath, heard his mother
calling his name. there was a bird in the house, it flew
in through the window. he got out of the bath to catch it
with her. he told me how they caught it and let it go.
i like to imagine the room covered in feathers like pillow fights
in the movies. he tells me she was beautiful, and i believe it.
i believe it looking at her wedding picture on my nightstand
that i stole from papa's room so long ago. i've always wondered
about the color of her skin and if her hair had hues of red
by her neck like mine does in the summer, but i've only seen
her in black and white. her name was hardeep, and i wonder
how she liked it. if she noticed how it rolls off the tongue
or if she knew it meant light. my parents stole the first three
letters for me, and it's heavy on my shoulders
to carry her name. heavy like the water in the bathtub.
heavy like cars on the road, like the one that crashed into hers.
papa tells me how they were going to rockefeller
center to see the christmas lights. i picture a boy of five
who looks like my brother in the backseat. he says he saw
her head, dented. i don't know where you go when you die,
but papa hopes she's watching us. he's felt her next to him,
he says he wishes she knew me. i tell him maybe she does.

years after she was gone, papa learned in english class
that when a bird flies into your house, it means something bad
will happen, it means someone will die. sometimes i wonder
if somehow and somewhere that long dead bird has feathers
that are still on the ground. still tainted by her fingertips.
not white like the feathers from pillow fights in the movies
but coated in dirt and mud and rainwater and maybe even

[...]

the scent of the lotion she used. when she caught that bird
and let it go, i wonder if following it ever entered her mind.
or if she thought about how you're never supposed
to touch a bird. or maybe she didn't think much about
it as much as we do. she's never seen that memory broken
and dissected. for her, it was just a bird and her little boy.
running and laughter and floors wet from bathtub water.
opening up the window and letting him go.

Prisha Rao

UNDYING MEMORIES

Some people say that when you die
you learn everything, you learn every little secret
and piece of knowledge in the world
I am hoping that my uncle learnt that his brothers still loved him
Even after fighting about money endlessly,
they never forgot to forgive him,
so I hope he knows

I found out and
I couldn't feel anything
I still cried knowing that I didn't want this to happen
Longing to feel something,
I started to think that the feeling of nothing
was the same as the feeling of death

His soul was just gone from the face of the Earth
This fact hit me
And the fact was that I wasn't ever going to
get to laugh talk and cry with him ever again
And most of all I felt pity and grief for my family and myself
This feeling felt better than nothing

My friends helped me up
And embraced me
They didn't even ask me while I sobbed
They just held me
as I muttered, "I didn't pray hard enough"
My thoughts continued cluttering around

It's probably going to be like this when I die or my sister dies
One of us has to deal with the other's death
Slip into the same thoughts that I did before

[...]

We slipped into it seven more times that year
I can still hear my mom saying
it's not an "eight sons and one daughter" family anymore
It's "one of us is dead"

THANK GOD FOR SHEEP

Thank God for sheep.
Thank sheep for wool.
Thank wool for blankets.
Thank blankets for warmth.
Thank warmth for us.

Gus Varallo

DEAR GALILEO

You hesitated
before stepping into the villa. Forced
only by the point
of my spear. You made
sure to close
the door
slowly, knowing you'd
never do it again.

When I patrol
your gardens I see
you, looking
out of the window, upwards beyond
the wooden
frame. You're a painting,
colored with the stars
and the Sagrantino vines
that surround you.

There is no God
here. Only trees
and ferns and even wineries
if you look far enough.
There's either hills
or plains, both strangled
by the tall grass.
There's an overgrown dirt
road to your courtyard.
There's my polished
spear, unworn. Recurring
rains, wasps, fresh rosemary
next to ivy, me trying to carry the weight
of watching your purgatory.

And there's you squinting
through the window, trying
to get through the underbrush
and back into the world.

Allison Wong

HIDE YOUR PEARLS FROM THE PIRATES

dear mom,
i've never been there
but you have
did you like it?
maybe not
because your parents took you and your siblings
        and you ran away
                on a boat.

dear mom,
it was claustrophobic,
you say
it was scary,
you say
you hid your pearls beneath your hair
you could not
        b
         r
          e
          a
           t
            h
             e
when they came in
you didn't know they would look like that
so normal,
you thought
pirates are real,
you say
and maybe we're all just ordinary
in extraordinary ways.

dear mom,
you were only seven
or eight
or maybe
even
six.

dear mom,
your parents took you to america
for more opportunities
my parents (that's you, by the way) took me to a small
suburb
so i would be safe
so, thanks for that

dear mom,
do you realize that i've never been there?
i should clarify
there means two places
china and vietnam
what's it like there?
if i go to beijing, will i wear an oxygen mask just
to walk the streets?
if i go to vietnam, will i know what war is like?

dear mom,
we're american,
you say
chinese and vietnamese, too
but i've lost those traditions
sorry

CONTRIBUTOR NOTES

Why do you like writing poetry?

Clara Collins: "Writing poetry is the only way to take a complex, huge, messy idea that I can't express and make it tangible. I love poetry because a poem never ends the way I imagined it would when starting. The reader and I discover something together."

E.E. Colmenares: "Poetry is a very personal and expressive form of writing that lets the author make known their true colors and feelings while still maintaining a guise. I like poetry because it lets me do that which I fight to do daily."

Bella Cosentino: "Poetry is a unique medium—its forms and lack of restraint give the writing a voice of its own. I can stumble in with a vague idea and be proud of the result in the end."

Emerson Davis-Martin: "I like to write poetry because it is a way to express myself. Growing up, I have tried to find different ways to show people who I really am as a person. I have tried singing and writing my own songs, and I tried playing the violin, but none of those things ever felt right to me. My mom is a writer and introduced me to poetry. I started writing at a time when I truly needed an outlet, and I continue writing to help me figure out who I am today."

Mya De La Rosa: "Writing poetry, for me, is an act of silencing a creature flapping about within me. On the page, the monster becomes something different, released from the recesses within me, and free to unsettle another mind some other day."

Nina Evans: "As an all-around creative, I enjoy expressing myself through many different media, often using music, prose, and art as my outlets. For me, poetry can be difficult to use, because I am such a maximalist in nature. However, I love to write poetry because it becomes a challenge; I have to learn to work with words in a pared-down setting while still carrying my idea through the poem. This is often why my poems surround the largest anxieties, hopes, or emotions in my life, because those subjects flow the easiest into my writing."

C.A. Harper: "I like writing poetry because poetry takes ideas and transfers them in a beautiful way to other people so they can play with the ideas however they want."

Elinor Koning: "I like to write about nature when I write a poem, and when I write I feel like my body is about to explode with thoughts. My ideas come mostly from where I live but also from my past and future. I'm proud of myself when my poem is down on paper and I read it to EVERYONE around!"

Sarah Lao: "I like to write poetry because there are no rules. If I want to cut out all the punctuation or make every noun a verb, I can, and if I want to spend two hours writing one line, I can. In that sense, it's very freeing. I can put all the emotions I'm usually not sure how to express into a set of images, and somehow, whether it should work or not, it does."

Cassidy Lewis: "To me, poetry is a way to use my head as an outlet for expression—inside I've always been able to find words and images that can be blended together to describe almost anything. Not only feelings I've experienced, but things I've seen and experienced, even the most mundane, can be poetic in different ways. Through poetry, I can look into others' heads too, and for a moment, see the world through a pair of eyes different from my own."

Layla Linnard: "I like poetry because there aren't rules to tell me how to express my thoughts and feelings. I get to use words how I want and that is exciting!"

Sarah Mohammed: "To me, writing poetry is not only an incredibly cathartic experience, but a way to convey messages of racism and misconceptions to others. Being a Muslim-American girl born to two immigrant parents who work very hard to rise in society, I relate to the stereotyping and profiling around Muslims, and I have learned to embody the grit and willpower needed to assimilate in this changing society. Poetry, to me, is a common language that helps to break boundaries in culture, religion, and gender to share our pain, anger, and experiences with thought that is deep and provoking. In a sense, poetry creates the magic in John Lennon's "Imagine"—where the man-made chasm of society doesn't exist, where there is no stranger, and instead we are one world of dreamers, more powerful than ever before, limitless with just a sky of hopes above us. I hope to raise awareness and embody the voice of change through my poetry."

Harkiran (Kiran) Narula: "I like writing poetry because I learn more about myself in doing so; I uncover feelings and thoughts that only writing can bring me to realize. Writing is the only way to sort out everything in my mind. To me, poetry is honest, raw and very vulnerable. Writing poetry is one of the only times I can be completely myself."

Prisha Rao: "Poetry is a piece of literary form of art that is usually up to interpretation. I feel as though some of my thoughts are ambiguous pieces of dough that can be open to interpretation as well. When I put these thoughts onto paper, they come easier out in the form of poetry. There are basically no limitations, so my writing can truly convey what I am trying to say."

Arthur Santos: "I feel really proud when I make up a poem. It is fun!"

Gus Varallo: "I always discover new things about myself when I write poetry. When I write poetry, I am able to define my values outside of the pressure of others, and the ability to do this gives me a greater sense of freedom and individuality."

Allison Wong: "I like to write poetry because it's possibly the most human way of expressing myself. It can be as simple or complex as I want, and it's still beautiful no matter what."

Some poets chose not to include a note.

Rattle Young Poets Anthology
Guidelines

1) Poems may be submitted by the poet, or the poet's parent, legal guardian, or teacher. Teachers may only submit on behalf of up to five students per year.

2) The author of the poem must have been age 15 or younger when the poem was written, and 18 or younger when submitted.

3) The poets may use their whole name, first name, or a pseudonym at their parents' discretion. We will not publish any contact information.

4) Submit up to four poems at a time.

5) Upon acceptance, a parent or legal guardian must sign a release allowing us to publish the poem. We will also request an audio recording of the poem by the child for inclusion in the ebook version and/or on our website.

6) Submissions will only be accepted through our Submittable portal. Include the parent/guardian's name and mailing address, and the child's age when the poems were written. The link to the portal can be found at:

www.rattle.com/children

Annual Deadline:
November 15th